L. Frank Baum

The Wonderful Wizard of OZ

Retold and activities by Jane Cadwallader

Illustrated by Gustavo Mazali

Young ELi Readers

2 Dorothy lives in Arizona with her Aunt Em, her Uncle Henry and her dog, Toto. One day Dorothy and Toto are in the house when suddenly ... WHOOOOSH! The house, Dorothy and Toto, go up up up in the air and fly away.

Aunt Em,
Uncle Henry
HELP!

Dorothy is in a magic land! The land of the Munchkins. The Munchkins are very happy because the Bad Witch of the East is under the house! But Dorothy wants to go home. She asks the Good Witch of the North for help. The witch tells her to find the Wizard of OZ.

The witch gives Dorothy the silver shoes of the Bad Witch of the East. Dorothy and Toto go along the yellow road to look for the Wizard of OZ. They talk to a scarecrow. He is sad. He tells Dorothy he isn't clever because he doesn't have a brain in his head.

Dorothy, Toto and the scarecrow go along the yellow road to look for the Wizard of OZ. They talk to a tin woodman. He can't move! He needs some oil. The tin woodman is sad. He tells Dorothy he can't love because he doesn't have a heart.

Dorothy, Toto, the scarecrow and the tin woodman go along the yellow road to look for the Wizard of OZ. They talk to a very big lion. The lion is sad. He tells Dorothy he isn't brave.

The five friends see the Emerald City.
This is where the Wizard of OZ lives!

They go to see the Wizard of OZ.
He looks different to each one!

But the Wizard of OZ says the same thing to all of them, first they must kill the Bad Witch of the West!

The friends go to find the Bad Witch of the West. She lives in the land of the Winkies. She only has one eye but she can see everything!
She puts on a magic hat. With this she can call the Winged Monkeys. She tells the monkeys they must kill the scarecrow and the tin woodman.

So the Winged Monkeys drop the tin woodman on some rocks and take all the straw out of the scarecrow and pick up Dorothy and the lion and take them to the Bad Witch of the West.

The Bad Witch of the West puts the lion in a cage and Dorothy has to do the housework. The Winkies are very sad! One day she takes Dorothy's silver shoe. Dorothy is so angry she throws some water on the witch and …

… the water melts the Wicked Witch like brown sugar! Dorothy and the lion are very happy! The Winkies are very happy too! The lion gives the magic hat to Dorothy.

Dorothy asks the Winged Monkeys to go and get the tin woodman and the scarecrow.

The Winkies mend the tin woodman and the scarecrow.

The Winged Monkeys take
them to the Emerald City.

They go to see the Wizard of OZ. But … oh dear! He isn't a real wizard!

The Wizard of OZ isn't a real wizard but he helps the scarecrow and the tin woodman.

And the lion.

He tries to help Dorothy too.
He wants to take her home in
a balloon but …

Dorothy is very sad! A soldier tells her to go and ask the Good Witch of the South. She lives in the land of the Quadlings. The lion gives Dorothy the magic hat to call the Winged Monkeys.

The Winged Monkeys carry Dorothy and her friends to the Good Witch of the South.

The Good Witch of the South points to Dorothy's silver shoes. She tells her to tap the shoes three times and say where she wants to go. Dorothy says goodbye to her friends.

She taps her shoes 3 times and ...

Hello Aunt Em. Hello Uncle Henry. I'm back from the land of OZ.

From where? Never mind, I am so happy to see you!

Activity Pages

1 **Who is who? Cross out the name that is wrong. Number the pictures in the order the characters appear in the story.**

~~Tin woodman~~

The scarecrow

The Bad Witch of the East

The Bad Witch of the West

The Good Witch of the North

The Good Witch of the South

Winkies

Munchkins

Uncle Henry

The Wizard of OZ

Winged Monkeys

Quadlings

2 **Match the pictures and the words and then write true sentences. Use the letters in the Wizard of OZ's bag and the picture dictionary to help you.**

Dorothy

The scarecrow

The tin woodman

The lion

WANTS A

WANTS TO GO TO

WANTS TO BE

WANTS A

h_a_t

Kansas

_ra_e

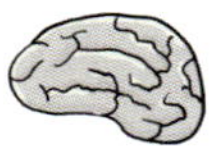
_ra_n

1 Dorothy wants to go to Kansas

2 ______________________________

3 ______________________________

4 ______________________________

3 Colour. Find the extra words. Make a sentence.

The points of the compass = blue
Parts of the body = red
Clothes = purple
Colours = green

4 Complete the sentences.

1 A  wears blue clothes.

2 A  wears ________ ________.

3 A  wears ________ ________.

5 Write *she*  or *he*. 

1 She is very bad.

2 ________ lives in the Emerald City.

3 ________ lives in the land of the Winkies.

4 ________ helps Dorothy's friends.

5 ________ calls the Winged Monkeys.

6 ________ only has one eye.

7 ________ isn't a real wizard.

8 ________ melts like brown sugar.

6 **Draw your favourite character from the story and write a description. You can choose some of these words to help you: *friendly, funny, good, happy, beautiful, young, old, short, small, big.***

My favourite character is ____________________

because ______________________________

____

____

7 **Do you like the story? Draw your face.**

= I love the story!

= I like the story.

= I quite like the story.

= I don't like the story.